OPTIONS TRADING FOR BEGINNERS

The Step-By-Step Crash Course to Make Money and Create a Passive Income By Options Trading Just a Few Minutes a Day

Robert Winston Moore jr.

Robert W. Moore Jr.
Trading Method

©Copyright 2020

TABLE OF CONTENTS

INTRODUCTION **1**
BASICS OF OPTIONS TRADING **3**
    What Are Options? 4
    Advantages of Options Trading 6
    Disadvantages of Options Trading 8
    Basic Terms to Learn 10

BASIC STRATEGIES FOR BEGINNERS AND HOW MUCH CAN YOU EARN? **16**
    Buying vs. Selling 17
    Comparing Short and Long Options 19
    Option Buying 23
    Option Selling 24
    How Much Money Can You Make? 24
    Long Call 27
    Long Put 30
    Short Call 33

THE BEST PLATFORMS AND TOOLS FOR OPTIONS TRADING **37**
    TD Ameritrade 37
    Tastyworks 39
    Robinhood 41
    E*TRADE 42
    Charles Schwab 43
    TradeStation 45
    Ally Invest 46

FINANCIAL LEVERAGE IN OPTIONS TRADING AND FUNDAMENTAL ANALYSIS – EVERYTHING THAT YOU NEED TO KNOW **48**
    How Does Leverage Work? 48
    How to Calculate Leverage? 50

What Is Fundamental Analysis? 53
Important Fundamental Indicators..............................54

TECHNICAL ANALYSIS VS. FUNDAMENTAL ANALYSIS – WHICH METHOD TO USE AND WHEN? 59

What Is Technical Analysis? 59
How to Get Started With Technical Analysis? 60
Common Technical Indicators for Options.................62
Key Differences Between Fundamental Analysis and Technical Analysis..67
Advantages & Disadvantages 68

CONTROL YOUR EMOTIONS LIKE A PRO – A STEP-BY-STEP GUIDE 71

Getting Started 73
Never Make Emotional Decisions 74
Be a Bit Math-Oriented...77
Maintain Trading Journals 77
Maintain a Disciplined Approach 78
Set Up Reasonable Expectations 79

OPTIONS TRADING STRATEGIES SPECIALLY DESIGNED BY EXPERTS FOR BEGINNERS.......81

Spreads..83
Strangles..88
Iron Condor 89
Naked Calls 93
Exit Strategies 94

AN EXAMPLE OF HOW OPTIONS TRADING WORKS 98

Case – 1 99
Case – 2 102

TIPS TO KEEP IN MIND IF YOU WANT TO BECOME A TOP TRADER.....................................105

    Know When to Improvise Your Plan 105
    Always Have Your Exit and Entry Plan Ready Before
    Starting 106
    Avoid Out-of-the-Money Trades............................. 107
    Don't Shrink Your Homework 108
    Don't Trade for Wealth But for Income 109
    Never Believe in Unfounded Tips 110
    Start With Enough Capital 111
    Don't Purchase Too Much With Margin 112
    Don't Keep All Your Eggs in One Basket 114
    Always Be Positive and Focused 114

HOW TO MINIMIZE YOUR RISKS? 116

    Diversify Your Portfolio 116
    Always Have a Plan 117
    Never Skip on Research 120
    Learn to Manage Your Emotions 121
    Always Keep an Eye on the Features Offered By Your
    Broker 123
    Manage Your Money Efficiently 124
    Always Monitor Your Trades 126

CONCLUSION 127

INTRODUCTION

Congratulations on purchasing Options Trading for Beginners: The Step-By-Step Crash Course To Make Money and Create a Passive Income by Options Trading Just a Few Minutes a Day and thank you for doing so.

The following chapters will discuss everything related to investing in options. Most people think that options are exotic but risky and that only those who have huge bankrolls can dare to invest in options. But this is completely wrong, and you are about to know why. No matter what type of investor you are, options are great for everyone. And I am saying this regardless of your individual risk tolerance. It is an amazing method to gain some profits from the stock market and also to level up your portfolios.

Even if you have a very small investment, with the help of options and the right strategies, you can increase it exponentially. Moreover, in the event of a market downturn, it is these options that will serve as a shield and an insurance policy for you. From the basics of options trading to the strategies you should use, in this book, you will learn it all. You will also learn how to implement those strategies in your own portfolio. By the time you reach the end of this book, you will have a complete understanding of the subject, and options trading will no longer seem an intimidating investment option.

There are plenty of books on this subject on the market, thanks again for choosing this one! Every effort was made to ensure it is full of as much useful information as possible; I hope you like it and that you will want to leave me a short review on Amazon; please enjoy!

Chapter 1
BASICS OF OPTIONS TRADING

This chapter is all about building a strong foundation before moving on to the advanced parts of options trading. There are some fundamental things that you should be aware of before trading, and all of these things will prepare you for the trade. It is true that there are many ways in which you can make money, and options are considerably more dynamic than any other method, especially when compared to stocks.

Now, you might be wondering why stocks and options

are different. Well, in the case of stocks, you are buying it at a certain price, and then you are waiting until the price goes up and reaches a certain level. This is when you are buying 'long.' And then, you sell that stock to make a profit. Or, you can also go 'short' when you are selling the shares you bought only to get them back later on at a price lower than what it was initially. But in the case of options, you can make profits in dozens of ways. This is because, here, we are not only speaking of stocks but also about several indices, commodities, and currencies. But before you trade options, you need to educate yourself properly, and only then you can maintain a comprehensive approach to the trade.

What Are Options?

Options are referred to as financial instruments. You can also call it a contract because when you purchase options, you obtain the right to trade the underlying asset of that option by a certain date at a specific price. But there is no obligation for you to do so. In short, an option is nothing but a security just like a bond or a stock. There are some defined properties and terms that strictly bind an option.

There are two types of contracts in the case of a stock option, and they are as follows –

- **Put Options** – In these, you have the right to sell the underlying asset within a certain timeframe at a specific price.

- **Call Options** – In these, you have the right to buy the underlying asset within a certain timeframe at a specific price.

No matter which type of option we are talking about, both of them have a predetermined price at which you have to either sell the option or buy it, and this particular price is termed as the strike price.

Another thing that is common in both options is the expiration date. This date defines the fixed timeframe within which you have to trade the option; otherwise, it will not have any value and will expire. If you want to make a profit, then you have to give the option to someone else before it expires. But there is another factor which you must know of, that is, the closer the option gets to the expiration date, the more it loses its value.

In usual cases, the date of expiration is the Saturday, which is the immediate successor of the third Friday in a particular expiration month. So, every third Friday of an expiration month is of importance to a trader. The expiration date of any option varies. For some, it can be as long as a year, whereas some can be short term, for example, a week. The most commonly traded ones last between thirty to ninety days.

The price of the option contract is denoted by the term premium. The conditions of the market keep affecting its value, and it also depends on the performance of the underlying security. The time value, when added with the intrinsic value, gives the value of the premium. Now, the time value depends on the time left until the expiration date. As already mentioned above, your time value will increase with longer time is left. Also, you will have to subtract the premium amount from the profit in order to sell the option.

Advantages of Options Trading

Here are some of the advantages of options trading that you should know of –

- **Lesser Financial Commitment** – When you are purchasing shares outright, you have to invest a lot of money, and on the contrary, the amount required to purchase an option is quite less than that. And I am not only talking about the premium but also the trading commission. So, you do not have to invest much upfront, and the money stays in your pocket so that when you make a profitable trade, the profit is of almost the same percentage as that of a stock trading.

- **Lesser Pitfalls For Option Buyers** – Whether you are buying a call option or a put option, you do not have to necessarily keep up with the trade. In case you turn out to be wrong about the trajectory of the stock or the time frame, you only lose that much amount of money as you paid for the trading fees and the contract. But for the option sellers, the pitfall is quite huge, and I am going to discuss that in the next section.

- **Greater Flexibility** – There are so many strategies open to investors to apply before the expiration date. They can expand their portfolio by exercising the option and then buying the shares. Or, they can sell all or some of the shares that they have bought. They can also choose to find another investor and then sell the contract of the 'in the money' options. Even if some of the money is lost on an 'out of the money' option, they can choose to get some of the money back by finding another investor before the expiration date and then selling it.

- **Ability to Fix a Price of the Stock** – In the case of options trading, the investors have the ability to fix a strike price. This means that before the expiration date, the investor will be able to sell or buy the stock at any given time at the strike price that they have set.

Disadvantages of Options Trading

Just like any other thing, options trading also have some disadvantages

- **Chances of Huge Losses for Sellers** – In the previous section, you saw that in case everything goes south, the buyer will not make many losses, but in the case of the seller, they can incur some huge losses. This is because whenever a call or put is written by an investor, they fall under the obligation to trade their shares no matter how unfavorable the conditions are before the expiration date of the contract. And now, you already know that the stock price can rise as high as it wants to.

- **Limited Time for Results** – The basic nature of options is that they have to play out in the short term. So, the investors are always on the lookout of a price movement in the short term that they can play out in their favor. And this movement should happen within weeks, or maximum – months. Sometimes, it even happens within days. So, there are two things involved. Firstly, the investor has to buy the contract at the right time, and secondly, they have to sell, exercise, or walk away before the expiration date of the option. But, on the other hand, stock investors can let their investments play out in years, and there is no deadline to worry about.

- **All Requirements Have to Be Met by the Trader** – For starters, you need approval through a broker before you can start to trade options. Here you will have to talk about your experience in investing, your financial means, and also your knowledge about the risks involved. After judging how you have answered all these questions, you will be assigned a trading level by the broker. The level that you are assigned will determine the type of options that you can trade. Your brokerage account should have a minimum amount of $2000 if you are trading options. This is a requirement that is set by the industry.

- **There Are Additional Costs** – Sometimes, you will have to make a margin account in order to exercise certain strategies. Now, this margin account is nothing but a collateral credit in case your trade does not happen in your favor. The margin account minimum requirement varies with the brokerage firm. In case the balance in the brokerage account falls below the minimum requirement, then you might get a margin call from the lender, and this means that your account might be liquidated unless and until you add more cash. Daily fluctuations in the market can easily lead your balance to fall below the minimum requirement.

Basic Terms to Learn

In order to complete the groundwork, you should understand each and every term, and so, here I am going to explain to you several key terms that are used very frequently in options trading.

Intrinsic Value

If I have to explain in very simple words, then I would say that the value of an asset is determined by the intrinsic value. There is a complex financial model and an objective calculation that is implemented in order to find the intrinsic value of an option. There are several meanings to intrinsic value, and it is based on the area of application. So, this is just an umbrella term. The strike price when subtracted from the price of the underlying security of the option when it is in the money, gives the measure of the intrinsic value. Here is an example to make it even clearer. Suppose the strike price of a call option is $25, and the stock underlying that option is being traded at $27, then the intrinsic value of that particular option is $2.

Extrinsic Value

The difference between the intrinsic value and the premium of a particular option gives the extrinsic value. In the above example, if the price at which the actual option is being traded is $2.50, then the extrinsic value is $0.50. There is another term that is used to denote the extrinsic value of an option; that is, time value.

In-the-Money

When an option has an intrinsic value, that is when the term in-the-money or ITM is used. In simpler terms, if you compare with the underlying asset's market price, then the value in the strike price is in your favor. These two points should make it even clearer –

- When the holder of the option has a scope of buying the underlying security at a value that is lesser than the present market price, then that is referred to as in 'in-the-money call option.'

- When the holder of the option has a scope of selling the underlying security at a value that is more than the present market price, then that is referred to as an 'in-the-money put option.'

You should also be aware of the idea of parity whenever you are talking about in-the-option. There is parity in the option if the intrinsic value is equal to the option price. Similarly, the option will be trading at a level above parity, when the price of the option is greater than the intrinsic value. When the option price is less than the intrinsic value, then the option will be trading at a level below parity. Usually, the options trade at a level above parity. Let us assume that the trading price of each share of an XYZ company is $100, then it will be trading above parity when the May 95 call is greater than $5(price of the option is greater than the intrinsic value). It will be trading at parity when the May 95 call is at $5 (the intrinsic value is equal to the option price), and similarly, it will be trading below parity if the May 95 call is less than $5 (option price is less than the intrinsic value).

At-the-Money

When the present trading price of an underlying asset is close to or the same as the strike price of the option, then it is called at-the-money or ATM. For example, if the trading price of each share of an XYZ company is $100, then the January 100 put, and January 100 call are at-the-money. Even if the per-share price is $99, then too the

January 100 put, and January 100 call is said to be at-the-money. But sometimes, the term 'near-the-money' is used to describe such a phenomenon. There is no intrinsic value associated with the ATM option but they might have a time value before the expiration date. In simpler words, when exercised, the ATM options are not in any position to fetch you a profit from the trade. But if the expiration date has not approached, then they still possess value. If you are guessing that there will be a huge stock movement, then the ATM options are going to be very attractive.

Out-of-the-Money

When an option is comprised of extrinsic value alone and does not possess any intrinsic value, that is when it is referred to as out-of-the-money or OTM. For example, if the trading price of each share of an XYZ company is $100, then the April 95 put and April 95 call are out-of-the-money. A put option can be termed as OTM when the strike price is less than the price of the underlying asset. Similarly, a call option can be termed as OTM if the strike price is above the price of the underlying asset. As compared to ATM and ITM options, OTM ones are not expensive. The reason behind this is that the ATM options can be called as possessing an intrinsic value since they are so close, and the ITM options do have an intrinsic value, but on the other hand, the OTM options do not have intrinsic value at all.

Implied Volatility

You will often come across this term in this book. It is a metric that will help you to understand whether the price of a security is under any likelihood to change. Implied volatility or IV is very helpful for investors because it will help you to understand and predict demand, supple, and moves in the future, and then, you can use it to set the price of your options contract. But you should also keep in mind that historical volatility and implied volatility are two different concepts. In the former, you will study the market changes that happened in the past and the results they brought. In bearish markets, there is an increase in implied volatility, and in a bullish market, there is a decrease in volatility.

Also, you will not be able to predict the direction of change with the metric implied volatility. For example, if you predict high volatility, then it means that there is a tendency of a large swing in price, but you do not know the direction of that swing. It can go very low, that is, downward and it can also go very high, that is, upward. The pricing of the options is hugely affected by implied volatility. Options are likely to be of higher premiums when they have a high IV and vice versa. But do not forget that the entire concept is based on probability, and there is no guarantee even though a lot of things are taken into account.

Chapter 2
BASIC STRATEGIES FOR BEGINNERS AND HOW MUCH CAN YOU EARN?

In this chapter, we are going to learn about the basic strategies that you can use in options trading. These are four in number – long put, long call, short put, and short call. This entire framework will be your foundation in the world of options trading, and once you get the hand of it, comprehending any type of strategy will become a cakewalk. Each one of these has been described in detail so that you face no problem in Chapter 7. But before we move into the details of the strategies, I am going to give you an insight into the process of buying and selling options.

Buying vs. Selling

Before performing any transaction in options trading, the first thing that you need to do is figure out in which direction the stock is going to move, whether it is likely to go sideways, higher, or lower. This prediction will help you to select the strategy that is best suited for that particular instance. You will learn more about how to predict this change in my next book – "Stock Market Investing for Beginners". Now, you will also have to keep in mind that there is a fixed expiration date for options, and this means that the time horizon will also have to be determined. This includes the underlying stock's move and how fast or how far it will move in a particular time horizon. Thus, the determination of multiple factors is required, namely timing, direction, and velocity of the underlying asset in order to come up with the best strategy.

If we are speaking in general, then whenever you think that there will be an increase in the volatility of the underlying stock or it will show a large movement, it is time for you to buy the option. Similarly, if you think that there will be a decline in volatility or there will be some movement within a fixed range, it is time for you to sell the option. You can also sell the option if you want to play the time decay in your favor. In this respect, let me remind you that the extrinsic value of the options will not remain the same over time, and it will decay, and that is the reason why options are also considered to be wasting assets.

Now, let us move on to the topic of buying vs. selling. The major difference between the two concepts is that when you are buying options, there is only one scenario in which you can make a profit at expiration, but when you are selling options, there are three scenarios at which you can make a profit. Here is an example to make it clearer.

Let us assume that in the month of February, ABC stock is trading at a price of $100 and let us say you want to make a February 105 call in order to buy or sell. If we ignore the premium, then it will be profitable when you purchase the call only if the price of the stock goes above the strike price of 105. But on the other hand, if you decide to sell the call, then at expiration, you will be profitable if the price of the stock rises above $100, moves sideways near $100, or even if it goes below $100. But the price should not go above the strike price of 105. The same situation applies to a purchase done at a 95 strike price put. You can make a profit if the price of the stock goes below the strike price of 95, but if you sell the 95 strike price put, then you can make a profit, if the stock declines, moves sideways, or rises.

Comparing Short and Long Options

If you have full confidence that the prediction you make on the magnitude and direction of the stock move is going to be true, then you can consider buying or going long on an option. Similarly, if you know that you can estimate a trading range and you also want to bring the statistical probabilities in the short term on your side, then you should consider selling or going short.

The strike price that you choose during a trade is one of those determining factors that will decide whether or not you make a profit. If the underlying stock finishes either below or at the call's strike price, then a short option can fetch you profit. Similarly, if the underlying stock finishes either above or at the put's strike price, then a short option will bring profits. You can structure a short option the way you want in order to ensure that you get a high chance of success, but there is a disadvantage too, and that is – the premium collected is relatively lower. Also, there is a chance that you might end up losing more money than the collected premium.

Here are some terms that you should be aware of before moving further in the book –

- *Delta* – It will show you the rate of change in the price of the option in comparison to a $1 change in the price of the underlying asset. You can definitely use the delta value while you are figuring out which options are best to sell and which are best to buy.

- *Theta* – If you want to measure the time decay of the option then you have to use the theta value. So, in simpler terms, it shows how much the price of the option decreases as the expiration date approaches.

- *Gamma* – This is used to measure the second-order price sensitivity or the change of the delta value of an option with respect to the price of the underlying asset.

The following table should help you understand the comparison in a better way –

Characteristic	**Long Put or Call**	**Short Put or Call**
Direction	If a call, then bullish; If a put, then bearish	If a call, then bearish; If a put, then bullish
Potential for	Unlimited	Limited only to the amount

profit		of premium collected
Debit or Credit	Debit	Credit
Delta	If a call, then positive; If a put, then negative	If a call, the negative; If a put, then positive
Theta	Negative	Positive
Gamma	Positive	Negative
Vega	Positive	Negative
Volatility	Positive when there is an increase, negative when there is a decrease	Negative when there is an increase, positive when there is a decrease
Time Decay	Negative	Positive
Risk	Only up to the premium paid	Chances of unlimited risk
Breakeven	If a call, then the premium paid along with the stock at strike price; If a put, minus premium	If a call, then the premium collected along with the stock at strike price; If a put, minus premium

	from the stock at the strike price	from the stock at the strike price
Advantages	Profit potential has no limitations; there is limited risk; leverage	The probabilities will be on your side; time decay
Disadvantages	Time decay; at times, can cost you more than what you want to pay; there is a chance that you might lose the entire premium amount	Risk is unlimited; the profit potential is limited
Profitable	The circumstances are narrow	There are multiple circumstances
Skills required	Correct on the magnitude, timing, and direction of stock	Correctly determining the trading range

Option Buying

If you want to make some profit from the stock rise, then you will have to purchase an in-the-money option. And with this, you can also utilize the benefit of leverage and, at the same time, have limited exposure to risk. On the other hand, if you purchase an out-of-the-money or at-the-money option, then you might rejoice at the lower cost, but you will also have to keep in mind that it means the underlying asset might not move fast or far enough. And then, you as a buyer might end up losing your money because of the factor of time decay. You always have to keep in mind that the extrinsic value is a friend to the option seller and not to the buyer because it exposed to time decay.

If you decide to buy a deep-in-the-money option, then it can be cost-effective if you want to trade the stock underlying the option, and the strategy is also risk-averse. For example, you can purchase a deep-in-the-money call if you think there will be an increase in the value of the stock. This will also help you to pay less as compared to the stock value, and at the same time, when there is an increase in the value of the stock, you will profit almost dollar to dollar. On the contrary, you should purchase a deep-in-the-money put if you think that there will be a decline in the value of the stock.

Option Selling

If you want to make a consistent and limited profit, then you can sell an out-of-the-money option. This will also help in putting the statistical probability in your favor. The maximum profit that you can make is the premium of the option, and this is fixed at the time of selling. So, you actually come to know what profit a particular transaction can bring you. In this way, goal setting as to the amount of money you want to earn every month can be easily set.

The first and foremost thing that you should figure out while you are selling an out-of-the-money option is that where this stock underlying the option will not go. For example, you think about where the prices of a stock will not reach when you try selling a far-out-of-the-money option. The act of determining where stock is not heading is much easier and simpler than determining where it is heading. Also, even if the prediction you made turns out to be wrong, you can still make some profit from selling options, but only if there is no drastic movement in the opposite direction.

How Much Money Can You Make?

One of the very common questions that almost everyone has is how much money is it possible to make with options trading. Well, if you ask me, then 10-50% of the trade or more is quite realistic if you play it well. So, if you have about $10,000 initially, then a profit of $250 to $1,000 could be made by placing the trades properly. Managing the risk in the right way is always a crucial step in making profits, and you will learn more about risks in detail in the latter part of this book.

Now, the truth is almost everyone wants to try their hands in the stock market, and if you are saying otherwise, then you are lying. Everyone has some dreams that they want to fulfill – it can be something like spending a year in Bali, skydiving in Dubai, or maybe buy an island in the Caribbean. Whatever it is, there is nothing wrong with that, but for every dream you have – the prerequisite is money that you cannot churn out from your monthly salary. That is probably the reason why people look forward to investing in stocks thinking that they will become a millionaire overnight. But there is no such thing as an overnight success.

In fact, you are asking the wrong question. Before you ask how much money you can make, you should be asking yourself how much time and effort do you want to put in trading options. It is true that the stock market can give you a sustainable income but not right at the beginning. Also, when people focus too much on earning huge amounts of money through the stock market, they often end up making the wrong decisions in the trade. Now, that creates the pressure of gaining back the lost money, which in turn boosts more bad decisions.

So, what you need to understand is that profits do not come in right from Day 1. You first have to learn a lot, and the learning ability of every person is different. Some people take time to learn, while some simply have a better aptitude.

Moreover, in order to make a sustainable income, you also need to practice discipline. You also need to learn risk management thoroughly because options are a risky endeavor, and there is a probability that you might lose your money if you do not treat carefully. You also need to have patience and then practice what you have learned through the various trading platforms. You also need to learn to control your emotions and not give in to panic in a stressful situation. The amount that you can earn through options trading also depends on how much cash you have kept reserved for trading. Also, you must only risk the amount of cash that you can afford to lose. You will learn more about these tips in the latter part of this book, but for now, I hope you have understood that what you can earn in options trading is highly subjective and depends on a lot of factors. So, there is no one-word answer to this.

Long Call

Now, we are going to discuss the basic options strategies one-by-one so that you can complete your groundwork. The long call strategy is probably one of the easiest and most basic strategies in options trading. In this type of strategy, the investor makes a prediction that the underlying security's price will go up significantly, and it will go above the option's strike price before approaching the expiration date, and thus, the trader decides to purchase call options.

Leverage

If you make a direct comparison with the shares underlying the option, then the buyer of the call option definitely has leverage because there is a faster appreciation in the value of the lower-priced calls (percentage-wise) for every point increase in the underlying stock's price.

But the lifespan of the call options is finite. If in case, the price of the underlying stock does not manage to go above the option's strike price within the expiration date, then it will no longer be of any use.

Profit Potential

When the expiration date approaches, there is basically

no limitation on the level to which the stock price can rise, so the profit that you can make from the trade also holds unlimited potential when applying the long call strategy.

Risk

The risk is very limited in the long call strategy. This is because it can only be up to the price that you have paid for the call option. This is irrespective of how low the price of the stock is trading as it approaches the date of expiration.

Breakeven Point(s)

The following formula is used in the calculation of the breakeven point that is reached at a long call position.

Breakeven Point = Premium Paid + The Strike Price of Long Call

Example

Now, to give you a better idea, here is an example –

Let us assume that the trading price of the stock of an ABC company is $40. Now, the strike price of a call option contract is $40 has its expiration date approaching in a month's time, and its price has been set at $2. Let's say that you think that the ABC stock will witness a sharp rise in price in the coming days and so you decided to invest a total sum of $200 to buy a single call option of $40, and it covers a total of 100 shares of XYZ company.

If what you predicted came to be true and let us assume that the new price of the stock on the expiration date becomes $50. Now, the price of the underlying stock is at $50. So, if you want to exercise your call option, then after buying those 100 shares at a price of $40 each, you can make a profit of $10 on each share if you sell them at $50 a share in the open market immediately. Since the number of shares in a call option is 100, the total amount that you receive after the transaction is $1000. Now, you had used $200 to buy the shares, so; the trade fetches you a profit of $800.

On the other hand, if you had predicted wrong and the price had dipped to $30 instead of $50, then the call option would have become worthless and expired. So, the money that you used to buy the call option, that is, $200, would have become worthless and incurred you a loss.

In this example, I showed you how the long call options could be implemented in the case of stock options, but remember, you can use the same strategy for options on futures, index options, and ETF options as well.

Long Put

This is also one of the basic strategies, just like a long call. In this case, the expectation of the investor after buying the put options is that the underlying security's price is going to go down before it approaches the expiration date, and it will go significantly below the level of the striking price.

Short Selling vs. Put Buying

Purchasing put options is a far more convenient way of betting against a stock than short selling the stock. This is mainly because, in the case of buying put options, you do not have to borrow the stock to short it. Moreover, the risk is limited because it gets capped to the amount you paid as a premium for the put options. But in the case of short selling, the investor will get exposed to unlimited risk.

On the other hand, the put options come with a finite lifespan, which is a major drawback. In case the stock price is still above the strike price before the expiration date is over, the put option will expire and become worthless. The stock price has to go below the strike price in order to make a profit.

Profit Potential

If you think theoretically, then on the expiration date, the stock price can reach zero, so the maximum amount of profit than an investor can make while using the long put strategy is unlimited. The profit can be calculated by subtracting the premium paid for the option from the strike price of the purchased put.

Risk

Now, the risk factor in the case of a long put strategy is limited. It does not matter how high the stock price rises before approaching the expiration date; the risk will always be limited to the premium you paid for the option. So, the maximum loss is obtained by adding the commissions you paid with the premium paid.

Breakeven Point(s)

In the long put position, the breakeven point can be calculated with the help of the following formula –

Breakeven Point = Long put's strike price – Premium paid for the option

Example

Here is an example to make the concept of long put strategy clearer to you –

Let us assume that the trading price of the stock of an ABC company is $40. Now, the strike price of a put option contract is $40 has its expiration date approaching in a month's time, and its price has been set at $2. Let us say that you expect the price of this option to fall steeply in the near future and so you decided to invest a total sum of $200 to buy a single put option of $40, and it covers a total of 100 shares of XYZ company.

Now, if your prediction turns out to be right and there is a severe crash in the price of the stock before it reaches its expiration date, the price falls down to $30 from $40. Now that the price of the underlying stock is at $30, the intrinsic value of your option, which is now in-the-money, will be $1000, and that is the amount you can sell it for. The amount that you paid for the purchase was $200, so this trade will fetch you a profit of $800.

But let us see what happens in case your prediction was wrong. If the price went up to $50 instead of going down to $30, the put option that you purchased would become worthless, and it will expire like that, which means that the amount you paid for the purchase, that is $200, will be your loss.

Just like the long call, this strategy can not only be used in the case of stocks but also for options on futures, index options, and ETF options.

Short Call

When you sell the call option because you know that in the near future, you will be obliged to purchase the underlying asset at a fixed price, it is called a short call. This strategy is used when the investor thinks that the price of the underlying asset is going to see a drop.

Profit Potential

The profit potential of a short call strategy is limited when the stock is traded at a level below the strike price. On the other hand, the investor can be exposed to high risks when the stock price rises and goes above the level of the strike price.

When to initiate this strategy?

When the investor predicts that there will be a moderate fall in the price of the asset, that is when the short call should be practiced for the best results. Even if the price of the underlying asset is at the same level, then too there would be a benefit. This is because you always have to think about putting the time decay factor in your favor. Over a period of time, when the call option approaches its expiration date, its time value will start reducing. Since you get an upfront credit, this strategy is quite a good one, and you will get the chance to offset the margin. But you should never forget that the strategy also exposes you to unlimited losses, especially if the price of the underlying asset increases dramatically.

Example

Now, let us move on to an example to understand the concept of short calls.

Let us assume that the trading price of the stock of an ABC company is $50. Let us say that you predict that the price of this stock will undergo a fall in the coming month. So, you write one call option with an expiration date in a month and its strike price at $53. The premium per share for the seller is $2, and since there are 100 shares in a call option, it will be a total of $200.

In case the stock price never increases above $53, the option writer will have $200 because of the premium, and the options will become worthless.

So, if you turn out to be wrong and the price of the stock rises to $55 before the expiration date, then you have to sell them at $53 instead of $55, which would bring you a loss of $2 per share.

Short Put

When a trader writes or sells a put option, it is referred to as a short put. The trader who buys the put option is long, and the one who wrote it is short. The premium is received by the writer of the put option, and that is the maximum profit that can be received. This strategy is also known by the name of a naked put or an uncovered put.

If a short put has been initiated by a trader, it means that they have predicted that the price of the underlying asset will not fall below the strike price and remain above it. The writer will be able to keep the premium if the price of the underlying asset remains above the strike price of the option, and the option will expire worthless. But if the price of the underlying asset falls below the strike price, then there are potential losses for the writer.

Risk

The risk in the case of a short put is unlimited even though the profit is limited. The premium received is the maximum profit you can make, but on the other hand, the risk is significant. The writer will have to purchase the underlying asset at its strike price when a put is written.

Let us say that the strike price of the put is $25, and the price of the underlying asset drops to $20, then the loss faced by the put writer is $5 for every share. This is actually less than the premium that they received. To realize the loss, they can close the trade, or they can also let the option become expired because of which they will own the underlying asset at $25.

But the writer will have to purchase the shares if the option is exercised, and this means there is a requirement of extra cash outlay. For every contract containing 100 shared, the trader will have to possess $2500 (100 x $25).

Chapter 3
THE BEST PLATFORMS AND TOOLS FOR OPTIONS TRADING

Since the times are quite volatile, choosing a broker for options trading is a very crucial step in order to make good profits. The list of platforms that I have provided here have been selected after extensive research, and they will also provide you with an extensive range of tools that will help you to manage and measure risk and assist you in placing profitable trades. Every platform is unique, and they all have some good points and bad points. Knowing the platform thoroughly is very important before you get started with them, and so, I have tried to provide you with a comprehensive approach.

TD Ameritrade

If you are just a beginner, then TD Ameritrade is really good for you. The platform is also trusted by several expert options traders as well. The reason why they are topping everyone's list is that they offer excellent resources for beginners, reasonable pricing, and lower commissions. It doesn't matter where you are in your journey of options trading; this platform has to provide a lot for everyone. Some of the notable features of this platform are as follows –

- TD Ameritrade had changed its system of commission in the year 2019. It was initially priced at $6.95 for every trade and a $0.75 extra for every contract. At that time, it was quite high as compared to the other brokers. For options trading, the platform only charges a fee of $0.65 for every contract, but this is a very typical rate when compared to other platforms.

- The charting feature of this platform is super good and advanced. In a few clicks, you will have a total analysis of real-time data. There are so many technical studies that you can access for every chart

- The trading tools are endless and impressive. With this platform, it is safe to say that the only limit is the sky. From replaying historical markets to conducting earning analysis, everything can be done on a single platform. They also have an option to conduct an advanced analysis of the options.

- The earning analysis tool will also help you measure the volatility. In simpler terms, it will make the entire process easier and will also bring clarity so that you can understand everything at once. And do you know what the best part is? With this platform, you will get data from Wall Street analysts at your fingertips.

Tastyworks

If you want to become a frequent options trader, then Tastyworks is the platform for you. The tools that are available on this platform are all about probability, liquidity, and volatility. As per the platforms, most of the trades that are placed on it are derivatives, and thus, their team is more inclined towards designing tools that will be of great help for options traders. Some of the features that you should know about are listed here –

- The process of opening an account on Tastyworks is probably the easiest thing to do. Once that is done, you will have to download the platform. One thing that I love about the platform that you can play around with the platform and check out its features before even funding your account.

- All the tools available on this platform are aimed towards helping you to evaluate the probability of profit and also evaluate the volatility.

- One of the key components of the platform is its watchlists, which you can access from the left-hand side of your device's screen. The watchlists are designed to be the same on the downloadable platform, web, and mobile.

- On the right-hand side of the screen, you will get options like alerts, activities, and position details. All the options can be customized based on what you want to see and what you don't. In the middle part of the screen, you will see that there is a trade ticket that remains open so that you can keep track of the transaction that you are constructing even when you are analyzing or charting any trade.

- You will get access to the latest trading ideas from weekly videos on the platform, and there is a huge library of pre-recorded videos as well.

- If you are performing options trades, then it is $0 per leg, for a contract to open a position, it is $1 per leg with $10 per leg being maximum. In order to close, it is $0. If you are performing a trade that has fifty contracts, then it would cost you ten dollars for every leg at the most. In case you choose to close the account, there is no fee.

Robinhood

If you are looking for a completely free platform, then you should check out Robinhood. After all, there is nothing cheaper than getting something for free. If you ask some of the professional options traders, then they will tell you that they do not like the trade handling process of the platform. But if you consider it for beginners, then the platform is really good, especially because it involves less risk. Since there is no amount of trading fee involved, you can basically sell options or buy them safely, and the only amount at risk will be what you invested initially. If you are just starting with options trading and want to you test the water, Robinhood is definitely a good place to start. Some of the features are as follows–

- The best thing about this platform is definitely the fact that it is 100% commission-free.

- You, as an investor, can start right now because there is no minimum account value involved. But yes, if you are purchasing an investment, you have to possess enough money for that. If you are opening a margin account, then the minimal portfolio value that you must have is $2,000.

- The entire process of opening an account on this platform is painless and is highly mobile-friendly. All you need is a few minutes, and you can get it done through the app itself. If you are approved, you will receive a notification within one hour.

E*TRADE

When you are just a beginner, E*TRADE can help you understand how you can improve the returns on your portfolio by trading derivatives. You will get proper guidance throughout your options trading journey. The mobile app is very much intuitive, powerful, and makes way for a smooth workflow. Here are some of the features that you should know about –

- There are two mobile apps available, and the platform has done some wonderful work this year to make its apps even more comprehensive and take the user experience to the next level.

- The Power E*TRADE website has a special tool known as Spectral Analysis, and with this tool, you will be able to assess the maximum amount of loss or profit that you will have for any particular options strategy. You will also get help in learning about the different risk metrics and how they can affect you.

- There is a paper trading function available with this platform that you can implement and test your strategies.

- If you want to place an order, it is extremely easy. There is a system of Trade Ticket, and you can even save the ticket for later. Across every platform, you will get the watchlists.

- In the case of options trades, the platform does not charge any per-leg commission. For most clients, the commissions for every contract are $0.65 whereas, for those who are placing more than thirty trades in a single quarter, the commissions are $0.50 for every contract. If the contracts have a price of $0.10 or even lesser than that, then any kind of fee is waived off.

Charles Schwab

The tools offered by Charles Schwab are robust and promising, and they will provide you with an all-round excellent service. Just like the desktop experience, mobile apps are fully featured. You can also exercise a high level of customizability on the platform. The features of this platform that you should know about are as follows –

- It is one of the very few platforms that will allow you to trade options without any commissions. A competitive contract fee is levied on options - $0.65 for every contract. But the amount is justified when you compare it with other platforms.

- The research offerings of this broker are probably one of the best that you will get. They not only provide earnings reports but also real-time news. There are multiple in-house experts who will provide you with market commentary and a large selection of research reports. You will also get access to a quarterly magazine, and you do not have to pay any extra charge for it.

- A Google Assistant is integrated into the platform, which makes things even easier for users because if you have any market-related query, you can simply ask Google. Apart from this, there is an Amazon Alexa skill too, through which you can not only create a watchlist but also get updates from it.

- Another good thing about the broker is that they do not have an account minimum.

- There are several platforms of this broker. For

options trading, they have the StreetSmart Central. You can also exercise mobile trading with them.

TradeStation

If you are planning to take options trading seriously, then TradeStation should definitely be one of your top choices. The TS GO offering of the platform was recently launched, which has zero minimum investment and trading costs. But you can also choose the TS Select plan where you can access the full range of tools, but it will also require an initial investment of $2,000. But there is one drawback, that is, you can access all the advanced tools only when you choose the TS Select plan. The pricing rules can be confusing too but there is no shred of doubt in the fact that the TS Select plan is quite comprehensive. Here are some features of the broker –

- The OptionStation Pro platform of the broker can be availed at free of cost. What is even better is that they have a preview mode through which you can create your own watchlists even on the mobile app, and you can keep track of the trends and charts even when you have not opened an account.

- If you want to get access to the comprehensive

research that this broker has, then you will have to go Premium. Once you do that, the TradeStation 10 platform will offer you more than 270 indicators. You can access historical data and then test your strategies by backtesting. And this data is huge because it comprises the daily data for the past ninety years. You will also get intraday data for the past decade.

- There are several free videos, tutorials, and ebooks available from where you can learn a lot about options trading.

Ally Invest

This is quite a low-cost brokerage, and they even have no account minimum. They are backed by Ally Financial. They can also offer you with a universal account management experience along with a website that is very easy to navigate. Some of the greatest strengths of this brokerage are as follows –

- hey have excellent customer service. So, if you are a beginner, Ally Invest is something you can rely on because they are so easy to use.

- In order to learn more, you can start with nominal investment, and you don't have to scratch your head about any big minimum fees or balance. You can take your time to learn since there is very low risk involved.

- Placing trades on this platform is a cakewalk, and you can modify settings, view the charts, and also conduct technical analysis like a breeze. There are as many as 117 technical indicators and 36 drawing tools at your disposal.

- The entire user flow process will be on a single page for options trading. Starting from the options chain, you will be directed to the strategy workbench from where you can move on to the probability calculator and then finally access the graph of profit or loss.

- The clean design of the platform makes it readable and easy to understand, and they offer in-depth market research too.

- The mobile experience of the platform is totally bug-free, and if you want to manage your portfolio, you need not worry because you will get access to the core functionalities from your mobile itself.

Chapter 4
FINANCIAL LEVERAGE IN OPTIONS TRADING AND FUNDAMENTAL ANALYSIS – EVERYTHING THAT YOU NEED TO KNOW

If you are into options trading, one of the most important concepts that you have to learn is that of leverage. Even if you have started with a little amount of capital, proper use of leverage will allow you to turn it into your favor and obtain significant profits. The usage of leverage is not always possible in the same way in every financial instrument, but in the case of options trading, the contracts act as a tool of leverage. With their help, you can expand your initial capital investment.

How Does Leverage Work?

Every option has an underlying security, and when you buy the contract, you gain control of that security. One such security is stocks. Now, if you had been trading stocks by themselves, then you would not have gained as much control as you would by trading options that have stocks as the underlying security. In simpler words, if you have a certain amount of money that you want to invest, then investing in options would definitely fetch you far greater profits than it would if you had invested in stocks directly. The main reason behind this is the fact that options contracts cost lower than the underlying security by itself but at the same time, the benefit you gain from the price movements of both are almost the same.

An example should make the concept clearer. Let us say you have $500 to invest, and you want to invest the amount in the stocks of Company X because you are predicting that there will be an increase in price. Now, if the stocks of Company X are being traded at $10, then with the money you have, you can purchase a total of 50 shares. If the value of the stocks goes up, then you can gain some profit by selling those stocks. For example, if they become $15, that is, there is an increase of $5, you will have a profit of $5 for every share when you sell them. The total profit that you will have in your hands is $250. But keep in mind that this does not take into account any commissions related to the trade.

Now, let us say that instead of stocks, you decided to purchase call options of Company X stocks. These stocks were being traded at $1, and the strike price was $10. So, if the size of the contract is 100, then at $100 each, you can purchase 5 contracts with your capital of $500. This means that you have control over a total of 500 shares of that company, with each contract having 100 shares. Now, if you compare with the previous example, you will notice that with the same initial investment, purchasing options gives you control of ten times the number of shares than what you had by directly purchasing stocks. So, when there is an increase in price to $15 for the shares of Company X, you would have made a lot more money than $250, if you had bought options and then sold them.

The example explained above demonstrates the importance of leverage and how it works. It also shows how even a meager amount of capital can allow you to make huge profits through options trading. This is also why so many beginners choose options trading. But if you want to learn more about leverage, you will have to know how it is calculated, which is what we are going to discuss in the next section.

How to Calculate Leverage?

In the example given in the previous section, you learn how there is a difference between investing $1000 in call options vs. directly in the stocks of Company X. You saw how options could give you ten times more control over the shares. But there is a common misconception that most people have. They think that having ten times more shares means that your leverage factor is also ten and that you will be making ten times more money from your investment. But that is not true.

When there is a change in the price of the underlying security, the price of the contracts undergoes a minimal change. So, an increase of $5 in the stock price does not mean that the price of the contracts will also go up by $5. In order to fully understand this relationship, you have to know moneyness and how it is related to the delta value (which is one of the Greeks).

Every contract has a theoretical profit built inside it, and the moneyness of that contract determines that profit. Moneyness is of three types, and we have already discussed in the previous chapter. These are – in-the-money, at-the-money, and out-of-the-money.

Now, let me explain the delta value. It is basically a ratio of the change in the contract price to that of the change in the underlying security's price. Suppose, the delta value of a contract is 0.5, then it means that its price would change $0.50 for every $1.0 change in the underlying security's price.

The contracts of the in-the-money options typically have a greater delta value as compared to the contracts of at-the-money options. They even have a greater value than the contracts of the out-of-the-money options. When you have completely understood all these details, calculating the leverage is pretty easy, and then you can even implement it while trading.

The leverage calculation goes something like this –

(Price of the underlying security x the option's delta value) / (Option price)

Now, in order to calculate the leverage, let us take the example that we had mentioned in the previous section. In that scenario, you bought at-the-money call options at $1 from Company X, where the strike price was fixed at $10, and the stocks of Company X were also trading at $10. Let us make an assumption that the delta value of these contracts was 0.5; then the leverage calculation would be something like this –

{Price of the underlying security ($10) x the option's delta value (0.5)} / {Option price ($1)}

Once calculated, the leveraging factor comes out to be 5. So, when you buy the options in place of directly investing in stocks, you will make five times more profit. But this calculation is based on the assumption that there will be an increase in price, and hence, you will make profits. The thing with the leveraging factor is that the factor applies in the same way for potential losses on your investment.

In simpler terms, the higher the value of the leveraging factor, the higher will be your chance of making handsome profits, but on the flip side, the chances of potential losses also become high.

What Is Fundamental Analysis?

Now, let us move on to one of the cornerstones of the finance world, that is, fundamental analysis. If you want to predict the future price of underlying securities, then understanding fundamental analysis is very important. There are several components that are studied here to perform an in-depth analysis of the market and not only understand the economy but also the company and the industry in which it operates. Once you have this data in your hands, you will be able to predict the future of market developments and also know what value does the stock of a particular company has. You will also be able to find out if a particular stock is undervalued or overvalued. If you are able to perform the fundamental analysis perfectly, then you will also be able to point out investment opportunities that others have not yet noticed.

Some of the components of a stock that are analyzed are as follows – competitor analysis, external politics, trade agreements, news releases, global industry, political conditions within the country, press releases of the company, and financial statements of the company.

If there is a bad impact on any of these fundamental indicators, then there is a possibility that the share price will be negatively affected. Similarly, if there is a positive change in the indicators, the stock price of that particular company will be boosted.

Important Fundamental Indicators

There is no wrong or right way to perform a fundamental analysis of a company because it is not like solving a mathematical problem. But there are certain performance indices known as fundamental indicators which are studied, and we are going to know more about them in this section. Although, you must understand that when different stocks or different industries show the same information, it does not necessarily mean the same thing.

EPS or Earnings Per Share

Every share of a company has its own portion of the profit that is denoted by the value EPS or Earnings Per Share. The profitability of a company is found out by its EPS. If you want to know whether investing in a particular company would be good for you or not, then you should check its EPS. The higher the value of the EPS, the better it will be for you. A healthy and stable company always has a higher EPS value. But you must also look out for any unusually high EPS value because that could mean one of these two things –

- The stock price will increase in order to make it at par with the earnings.
- There might be a decrease in the earnings, and then the level would go back to normal.

P/E Ratio or Price-to-Earnings Ratio

Every company has its own payouts, and the ratio of those payouts as compared to the stock price is what the P/E ratio or the price-to-earnings ratio denotes. So, when compared to the price of the stock, you will know whether a share of that stock will pay you well or not. Now, you must be wondering how you can calculate this ratio. It is quite easy. All you have to do is divide the price of each share with the earnings from each share. So, let us assume that the price of each share of a company X is $20 and the earnings of that stock per share is $2, then the P/E ratio is (20/2)=10

The earnings will be high compared to the price of the stock when the P/E ratio will have a lower value. Usually, the stock will be more attractive when the P/E ratio is low. But there can also be extra potential when the levels of P/E ratio are unusually low. So, if the P/E ratio is low, as in less than 10, then you can say that the particular stock is undervalued. So, you can predict a price increase. Similarly, the opposite happens when the P/E ratio is high.

P/B Ratio or Price-to-Book Ratio

This ratio measures the value of a stock in comparison to the company's book value. If the outstanding shares of a company are 500,000 and it has a worth of $10 million, then the book value for every share is $20 (10 million/500,000). Now, let us consider that the trading price of each share is $80, then the P/B ratio will be –

80/20 = 4

It is believed that when the value of the P/B ratio is more than 1, then it means that there will be faster growth in the stock, and that is also why the stock price is much high as compared to the book value. Sometimes, values like 100 or even more than that are seen for the P/B ratios of certain companies.

ROE or Return on Equity

When the company uses the shareholder's equity, its efficiency is measured by the ROE or return on equity. The shareholder's equity, when divided by the net income of the company, gives the ROE value. If a total of $5 million income has been generated by the company this year and the value of shareholder's equity stands at $50 million, then the ROE will be 10% ($50 million/$5 million). The ROE is always considered in the form of a percentage. The efficiency of the company is measured in terms of the ROE. The higher the value of the ROE, the more efficient the company is.

Beta or β

If you want to find the correlation between the price of the stock and the industry in which that particular stock operates, then you will have to look for the beta value. The stock is compared to a benchmark index to find this value. The value usually falls between -1 and 1, but there are certain instances when the value of beta might not be in this range. The correlation is higher if the beta value is more than 0, but with a high beta value also comes an increase in volatility. In simpler terms, the risk associated with the underlying assets in that option also increases.

I have already mentioned some of the best platforms for options trading in Chapter 3, but here, I am going to mention those platforms which are currently the best in the industry for performing fundamental analysis.

TD Ameritrade

This is definitely going to be my first choice owing to the wide array of tools they have, and their research section is very much comprehensive. They even provide you with a stock screener through which you can customize your own fundamental parameters and then filter the stocks based on that.

Yahoo! Finance

They are one of the oldest platforms, and they still have a very good range of fundamental stock data. There is a search bar on their platform through which you can search for what you want. There are a lot of options related to statistics, financial reports, and historical data.

Chapter 5
TECHNICAL ANALYSIS VS. FUNDAMENTAL ANALYSIS – WHICH METHOD TO USE AND WHEN?

In the previous chapter, we learned about fundamental analysis, and here, we are going to see what the differences between technical and fundamental analysis are. But first, you need to have a basic idea of what technical analysis is.

Are you enjoying this book? if so, I would like to know the opinion of my readers, you can leave me a short review on Amazon, I would be happy! Thank you

What Is Technical Analysis?

If you want to fully understand and predict what the entry and exit points in the market should be, then understanding technical analysis should be your first and foremost priority. Fundamental analysis is all about making decisions based on industry trends, valuation, and revenue. On the other hand, technical analysis is about volume and price from historical data. In this method, investors implement behavioral economics and statistical analysis so that they can bridge the gap between market price and intrinsic value.

In technical analysis, there are two different approaches, and it is important that you choose the right one for yourself –

- **Top-Down** – This approach is more about macroeconomic analysis. This means that this approach is less about individual securities and more about the overall economy. The primary focus will be on the economy, and then the focus will shift to the various sectors and then finally to the companies present in those sectors.

- **Bottom-Up** – The next one is just the opposite, where the investors focus more on individual stocks rather than a macroeconomic analysis. If a particular stock seems interesting, then this approach will help in finding the possible entry and exit points in that stock.

How to Get Started With Technical Analysis?

If you are just a beginner then here are some of the basic steps that you should implement in order to get started with technical analysis –

- **Develop a trading system** – This is the first step, and it means you have to identify a technical analysis strategy that works for you. For example, if you are a beginner, then you might go for the moving average crossover strategy. In this method, you will be keeping track of the two moving averages on any particular stock's changes in price.

- **Find the right strategy for your tradable security** – Not every strategy is meant for all securities. If your tradable securities are options, then you have to find the strategy that fits it. Sometimes, the parameter choices also start changing with the security you choose.

- **Choose the right brokerage account** – The next step is to choose the right brokerage account where you will be able to trade the type of security you have chosen. Not every brokerage account gives you the tools needed to perform technical analysis of options. The brokerage account you choose should have proper monitoring and tracking functionality with the technical indicators you need. Also, you need to make sure that your costs are low so that your profits are not affected.

- **Choose an interface to monitor trades** – Depending on the strategy you have chosen, the functionality you need also changes. So, choose your interface carefully.

- **See whether you need any more applications** – Sometimes, in order to maximize the performance, you might need other applications too. Some traders prefer trading on the go, and so they look for platforms that would give them mobile alerts. So, if there are any such special requirements, think whether you need any more applications to support you.

Now, technical analysis for options trading is slightly different mainly because there is the subject of time decay in options. You cannot hold a position for an indefinite period of time. There is an expiration date for every option before which you will have to leave it. So, some of the common technical indicators that are used in this case have been discussed in the next section.

Common Technical Indicators for Options

Since options trading is a form of short-term trading, some of the things that you can determine with the help of technical indicators are as follows –

- The direction of the movement
- Range of movement
- Duration of the movement

RSI or Relative Strength Index

This is basically a momentum indicator, and with the help of RSI, you can measure the magnitude of the losses and gains incurred over a certain period of time and then compare them so that you can find out the change of price movements and speed of movements of a security. This will, in turn, help you point out oversold and overbought conditions. The value of RSI is usually between 0-100, and overbought levels are indicated by an RSI value over 70 and oversold levels are indicated by a value less than 30.

When options are based on individual stocks that is when the RSI values perform the best as compared to indexes. If you want to perform short-term trading by looking at the RSI value, then options on high-beta liquid stocks are what you should look for.

Bollinger Bands

I have already spoken about volatility time and again throughout this book, and in order to measure volatility, Bollinger bands are one of the best ways to do so. When there is an increase in volatility, these bands increase, and similarly, when there is a decrease in volatility, these bands contract. When the price moves so as to become close to the upper band, that is when it suggests that the security might have been overbought. On the contrary, when the price moves so that it becomes close to the lower band, that is when it suggests that the security might be oversold.

You can predict a reversal when you see a price movement outside of these bands. And predicting all of these definitely helps the option traders to position themselves in the correct manner. For example, if you notice that there is a breakout above the top band, then you can initiate a short call or a long put. On the contrary, if there is a breakout below the lower band, then it can be predicted as an opportunity for a short put or long call.

You must also not forget that it is the periods of high volatility when you should be looking forward to selling options in order to make profits because this is when the prices of options are elevated. Similarly, when there is low volatility, you should consider buying options because the prices of options are on the lower side.

IMI or Intraday Momentum Index

If you are a high-frequency trader and if you want to start

trading on intraday moves, then the IMI will prove to be a great indicator for you. The concepts of RSI and candlesticks are combined in this particular technical indicator. With the help of this strategy, initiating a bullish trade becomes easier, and you will be able to spot the possibilities where you can do so in a market that is trending upwards. Similarly, the technical indicator will also help you to initiate a bearish trade in a market by spotting the right possibilities in a market that is trending downwards.

MFI or Money Flow Index

Both the volume and price data are combined in this particular index, and that is also the reason why this is sometimes known as volume-weighted RSI. The outflow, as well as the inflow of money into an asset when considered over a period of time (for example, two weeks), can be measured by this technical indicator. This indicator is also an indicator of trading pressure. You will know that a particular security has been overbought if the MFI value is above 80. On the other hand, you will know that a particular security is oversold if the MFI value is below 20.

Since MFI depends so much on the volume, it is better suited for options trading done solely on stocks and also the ones that are done for a longer duration of time. You can predict a change in the trend if you notice that the stock price and the MFI are moving in opposite directions.

OI or Open Interest

Any unsettled or open contracts in options are indicated by the OI or Open Interest technical indicator. But keep in mind, that this technical indicator does not necessarily denote that there will be a specific downtrend or uptrend. You can find out the strength of a certain trend with the help of this technical indicator. You can predict the inflow of new capital when there is an increase in OI. This also indicates that the existing trend is going to sustain. Similarly, you can spot a trend is weakening when the values of OI decrease.

PCR or Put-Call Ratio

With the help of this particular technical indicator, you will be able to get an idea of the trading volume by comparing the call options with the put options. If there is a change in the overall market sentiment, it can be predicted by a change in the value of PCR.

The PCR value is more than one when the number of puts exceeds the number of calls. This means it is a bearish market. Similarly, the PCR value is less than one when the number of calls exceeds the number of puts.

This means that it is a bullish market.

Key Differences Between Fundamental Analysis and Technical Analysis

- If you are looking for a more long-term approach in analysis, then it is fundamental analysis because, with its help, you can figure out which stocks are about to witness a rise in value in the upcoming days. Technical analysis is more of a short-term approach, and that is the reason why it is more relevant for options trading and day trading. In this, you will get to know which stocks can bring you profit if you buy them now and then sell them in the future at a higher price.

- Investing is the main objective of fundamental analysis since it is all about the long-term. But trading objectives form the core of the technical analysis.

- The intrinsic value of a stock is something that is put to use in the case of fundamental analysis so that in the long term, the profitable stocks can be identified. The past performance of stocks is taken into account in the case of technical analysis so that its price movement for the future can be predicted from that.

- Both present and past data regarding a stock are considered in the case of fundamental analysis. Only the past data is considered in the case of technical analysis.

- Financial statements and data are analyzed to make decisions in fundamental analysis. Price movement trends and charts are analyzed to make decisions in the case of technical analysis.

- There are no assumptions when you are performing fundamental analysis. You will have to make several assumptions in technical analysis. For example, you may have to assume that the price will follow a similar trend as it did in the past.

Advantages & Disadvantages

For Fundamental Analysis –

Advantages:

- Only sound financial data are used to perform fundamental analysis. Thus, there is no scope of personal bias anywhere.

- You will arrive at a proper recommendation to either buy or sell by using analytical and statistical tools.

- Several long term trends of demographic, economic, consumer, and technological origin are considered.

- Rigorous financial analysis and accounting pave the way for understanding everything in-depth and leaves room for no mistakes.

Disadvantages:

- When you are considering the financials, some assumptions have to be made. So, I always advise everyone to consider both the worst and best scenario. There can be unexpected legislative or economic changes at any time.

- The entire process of industry analysis takes up a lot of time, and it is definitely not a cakewalk.

For Technical Analysis –

Advantages:

- You come to know the possible entry and exit points in the trade.

- You get to know how the overall market is performing, and you can judge the overall sentiments that are running.

- When you notice patterns, you can predict directions of movement.4

Disadvantages:

- The underlying fundamentals are not taken into consideration while performing technical analysis. And thus, several risks can crop up because of this.

- Sometimes, if your chart is full of too many indicators, then the signals can be confusing.

Chapter 6
CONTROL YOUR EMOTIONS LIKE A PRO – A STEP-BY-STEP GUIDE

Since trading options is mostly about short time periods, most people have this idea that the prices of options are not going to fluctuate much in that time. But that is wrong, and you need to rethink if you are thinking along those lines as well. If you study past data, you will see that options trading witnesses a lot of fluctuations in price even if it is over a short period of time. So, if you think that options trading means your money will stay protected, then I have to tell you that you are wrong. Of course, people lose money in options trading, just like investing directly in the stock market. But that does not mean you have to be happy about the fact you are losing money because you will feel low and you will start panicking – that is the NORMAL reaction. But you have to learn how to keep your emotions in check.

You need to learn how to remain calm and observe your emotions from a distance instead of giving in to them. Slowly, you will learn how you can stick it out so that you can see whether or not you get any good returns in the future before the expiration date. Options trading can really be a financial roller coaster. You cannot invest in options with the mentality of a Warren Buffet investor because options do not appreciate in the same manner. A little bit of study would reveal that options increase on a percentage basis, and their movement is way faster than any other type of investment.

For example, if a person has multiple contracts in his/her possession and is trading them all, then they might incur simultaneous losses and profits of $500 each over the course of a few hours. But technically speaking, do not confuse options traders with day traders because they are not, but your mindset should be slightly like that of a day trader if you want to make it big in options trading.

In this chapter, I am going to show you how you can control your emotions even when you are on this rollercoaster ride of options trading.

Getting Started

As a beginner, you will have a tendency to jump into the market right away and begin your journey as a trader. But before you do that, let me remind you of some of the things that are crucial for you to learn. I cannot stress enough on the fact that a good and proper understanding of the basics of options trading is going to get you far in your journey. You also should learn about the different types of options that are present in the market so that you know what you should pick. I know that I have probably told you all of this before, but I am reiterating this for one simple reason, and that is – this is the golden rule about being a top trader. The more you enhance your knowledge about investing, the more will be your chances to get success.

Once you have gone through all the basics and understood them carefully, you will have a clear picture in your head about what you are getting yourself into. The next step is to find your motivation and always hold tightly to it because, in trading, beginners tend to lose that motivation very fast. You need to ask yourself exactly how much money do you think about making.

The figure will vary from person to person, and although there is no limit to this, you should still be realistic about it. No one becomes a billionaire overnight. You should also ask yourself how you plan to spend or use that money once you have earned it. This is where you are going to find your motivation because you are setting goals or you have some dreams that you want to fulfill, and so you will try your best to make those dreams come true. When you are in the thick of the trading, this motivation is going to keep you going and also help you stay focused on the trade.

When you have the trading plan ready, it will constantly tell you about the things that you should achieve in a trade. Some of the common things that are included in a trading plan are – your goals, your idea of what is going to happen, the strategies that you want to use, and any other note or guideline that you think might be of use to you. All of this together is going to make you successful. You will be putting yourself into a risky endeavor if you start trading without having this plan ready.

Never Make Emotional Decisions

As you must have understood by now that options are very volatile in nature, and depending on certain stocks, it can get really very volatile. There are so many beginner traders who come into options trading but then become emotional because it is not what they thought it would be. And this is exactly what I am talking about. This approach will not do any good to you, and that is why prior research is necessary to know the waters you are stepping into.

In most cases, people exit at the wrong time just because they became emotional and overwhelmed during the trade, but only if they had stayed a bit longer or if they had made their exit a bit early, they would have been able to make a lump sum profit. If you are trading options, your worst mistake would be to make any sudden moves. That is why a trading plan is so necessary so that you can have all the rules at hand on when do you need to exit or enter a trade. And all you have to do is stick to those rules.

The tides in the financial market keep changing, and if you want to navigate them like a pro, then active monitoring is important. There will come a time when you will feel like giving in to your behavioral impulses, but you have to stop yourself right there and take a step back to analyze the situation in front of you. The market ups and downs can easily make you start practicing emotional buying and selling if you are not careful. And the usual trend shows that whenever the market is good, investors have the tendency of piling into investments and then they sell at the bottom. This is mostly because of the fear and hype generated by media.

There are several theories that have been proposed about investor behavior because it is something that is being studied extensively. But if we look at the real-life situation, you will understand that trading can bring about stress, and in situations of extreme stress, it is quite common for rational thinking to be clouded by the investor's psyche. The stress can not only be a result of panic but also euphoria. That is why I have told you time and again that the approach towards investing should be realistic and rational. Never underestimate risk management because every investment has its own risks, and if you do not gauge those risks, then you are the one who will be at a loss.

There are so many non-professional investors in the market who actually use their hard-earned money for trading just because they think they are going to receive a huge return. But sometimes market developments can lead them to lose their money, and it is very painful indeed. All of this leads to extreme stress and that stress, in turn, can lead to second-guessing every step. That is why you need to identify what your risk tolerance is so that you do not end up making emotional decisions when these risks become unbearable for you.

Be a Bit Math-Oriented

If you are not good with numbers or if you are shy about it, then you are not going to do well in options trading. This is because it is entirely a game of numbers. But don't get me wrong, I am not asking you to go to some renowned university to get a degree in mathematics or statistics. You can read a bit by yourself and get a grasp on the basic concepts because a little bit of knowledge about statistics and probability will do you good in the long term and make you better than the others in the world of options trading. To be honest, I don't know how you are going to get to the top if you do not know the basics of statistics. The core of options trading will always have some Maths in it, and you cannot go around it in any way.

Also, when you are math-oriented, you will have a better understanding of the market, and you will see options in a different light. You will learn to analyze the situations and markets before going all-in with your capital. This, in turn, will also make strategizing an easier process.

Maintain Trading Journals

When you have a trading journal, keeping track of your trade becomes way easier. Your brokerage statement is not going to include everything, whereas your trading journal will have all those details, making it easier for you. It will also remind you of the mistakes you made in a certain market condition. Do you know how this is going to benefit you? If that same market condition were to repeat itself, you know exactly what strategy you will not be using, and this will help you not to make the same mistake again. You can also keep track of every time you became emotional and what triggered you. This is will not prevent you from becoming emotional but it will remind you of the loss you incurred and this probably will help you get a grip on yourself.

When you record your trades and make notes in your journal, you get a clear picture of the situation you are in. Yes, sometimes, that picture can be bad, and this does not mean that you have to back out. A losing record is simply when you have to find out where you are going wrong and why you are not making profits from the trade. All of this will become easier because you have written your steps in the trading journal. And then all you have to make is adjustments.

Maintain a Disciplined Approach

You must be wondering what I mean by a disciplined approach. Well, I simply mean that don't invest your money in options just because you have a feeling about them or you think they make you feel good. No! That is just gambling and nothing else. Before investing, you have to perform thorough research. This means you have to perform fundamental and technical analysis, as mentioned in the previous chapters. You have to pay attention to how the stocks performed in the past years and also be aware of what its recent history is.

Also, most beginners do not revisit their trades once they have closed it. Don't do that. Even if you have made a profit from a trade, revisit it at some other time to see if there were any improvements that could have been made and then make a note of that because it will help you in your future strategies when similar market conditions arise.

You should never blame the market for anything because it is simple blame-shifting and nothing else. If anyone is responsible for the losses you incurred, then it is you. That being said, you do not have to beat yourself up emotionally if you made a loss. You have to learn from it, get up, and not repeat the same mistake again.

Set Up Reasonable Expectations

This is probably one of the most important points when it comes to controlling your emotions in a trade. It is good to aim high, but you should also judge the market conditions before aiming too high because that might be unrealistic for the market condition you are presently in. Also, if you are new to the market, then it is advisable that you start with normal expectations. In fact, you should prepare yourself mentally that you might lose your capital so that in case you lose it, you will be prepared for it emotionally.

Once you have a market experience of about a year, then you can start setting expectations. If you want to be an achiever, you need to be patient. When you have unreasonable expectations, it is most likely that you will not be able to meet them, and that is when you get hit emotionally. This causes stress and panic and leaves a devastating effect on future trades. You make wrong decisions, or you are too scared and exit trades early missing out on profits.

Now that you know the steps you need to take to control your emotions, there is one last thing that I want to say, and that is – success can only be achieved by hard work and nothing else. There is no shortcut to it. You need to have a proper plan, and you also need to have the patience for that plan to work out. No matter what is happening in your life or what your mood is, you cannot let these things affect the trade. If you think that something in your personal life is bothering you too much, then take a break and sort it out first before proceeding with the trade.

Chapter 7
OPTIONS TRADING STRATEGIES SPECIALLY DESIGNED BY EXPERTS FOR BEGINNERS

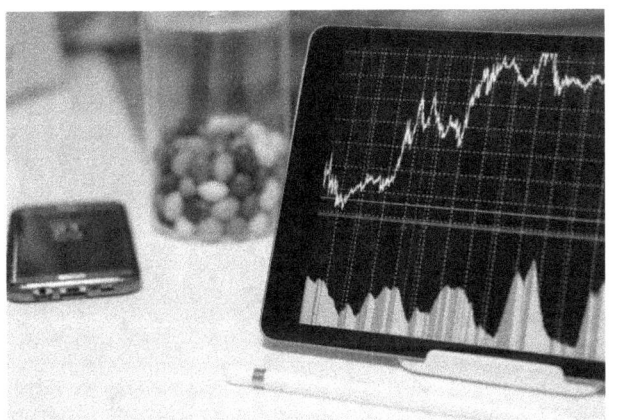

Risk is a major part of almost every sector and not only options trading. But when you have a good strategy with you, these risks can be effectively minimized, and you will also be able to pinpoint the right investment in a particular market condition. You will also know when to enter the trade and when to exit it with the help of these strategies. This, in turn, will help in maximizing your profit. There is a pattern that most investors who have just started their journey in options trading have failed because of one thing, and that is – they did not choose the right strategy. Or, they chose the right strategy but they were not aware of the procedure in which they should use it.

When you have the right strategy with you, you will also make the right decisions regarding which options to choose. It is also true that not every strategy works well with every option, and that is you start with the strategy, and then you select the option and not the other way around. When you are just starting out, it is normal for things to seem a bit complicated. But in this chapter, I am going to explain to you certain strategies which have been specially designed by experts for beginners like you and these chapters will help you navigate the market like a pro.

Over time, you can choose to mix and match the strategies that you have learned. There are different prerequisites for the different options trades, and so you do not necessarily have to be stuck doing the same thing over and over again. There will be changes in the market condition, which will also require a change in strategy. If you are in the same trade then you can keep using the same strategy but if you are changing trades, then you should always check other strategies and see whether you need to switch things a bit to maximize your profit potential.

So, here are a few strategies that every trader should know –

Spreads

When there are two transactions involved, especially those which are executed at the same time, the spread strategy is used. The strategies that we covered in Chapter 2 were the most basic that lay the foundation of options trading, and now the spreads are the next step that a beginner should take. Vertical spreads are the most common, and in these, the strike price of one option is higher than the other. There is a term 'leg' that is used to refer to each transaction in the spread. One of the biggest advantages of this type of strategy is that the potential losses and risks are minimized. But the major disadvantage is that your profit potential also gets limited in this type of strategy.

Bull Call Spread

Bullish investors are the ones who use this type of strategy. This is a type of vertical spread. In this strategy, the call options for a particular stock are first bought by the investor at a certain strike price, and then, at the same time, for the same stock, a call option is sold at a strike price that is higher than before. The expiration date for both the options, in this case, would be the same.

Bear Put Spread

This is another type of vertical spread and is meant for bearish investors. These investors predict that there will be a decline in the price of the stocks. Here, the put options are bought at a strike price, and then, at the same time, all of those put options are sold at a strike price lower than before. The underlying stocks, in both cases, have the same expiration date. If you are looking for a strategy that doesn't involve short selling the stock, then the bear put spread is what you need.

Time/Calendar Spread

The last two strategies involved options that had the same expiration date, but here it is going to be different. In this strategy, an option with a certain expiration date is purchased, and then it is sold at another expiration date. What remains the same in both these cases is the strike price. The core idea of this strategy is to take full advantage of the factor of time decay.

Butterfly Spread

These are a bit complicated that the rest of the spreads and so I am not going into the details. I am simply mentioning it to tell you that this is another type of spread strategy that is there, and it is basically a combination of the bear and bull strategy. Another thing to note is that there are 3 different strike prices involved.

If you want to know more about these advanced strategies, then you should check out my second book on *Options Trading* where I will further explore them in greater depth.

Straddle

In this type of strategy, the investor is not really invested in any side of the market, and you call it a type of combination trade. Even the type of trade is not a concern here. It can be bearish or bullish – it does not really matter. But what matters is that you have to avoid the sideways market at all costs. There must be some direction working in the market, and you don't have to worry about anything else. You only need to monitor the force at which the market is moving in that particular direction.

At the same time, there will be an increase in value for the other leg of the trade. But you have to remember one thing here. The value you pay for the leg that is unprofitable is the amount by which the breakeven point will move. Thus, your main aim should be that the profitable leg should also move by the same value as mentioned before. So, the skill you need to master is probability, and you have to determine the probability of the stock moving in either direction. Your accuracy would lead to your success.

In order to give you better clarity on this matter, let us take a step back and assess the situation. As we already know, when a stock shows movement in a particular direction, the degree by which it moved is determined by volatility. If you want to understand and learn about the market's current state of volatility, then you should check the VIX, which is a very popular chart meant for exactly this purpose. I am asking you to see this chart because you will not have to trouble your mind with things like how these numbers are calculated. Once you have moved on to an advanced stage of trading, then you can think about the calculation of volatility numbers.

What you need to focus on now is when the stocks show a degree of greater volatility within them. One of the best examples of this scenario is when earning announcements are done. Under-performance and over-performance is often a result of earnings announcements of companies that are highly anticipated. This is also why there is a steep change in stocks, both in negative and positive directions. Another similar effect is caused by the results declared after elections.

The volatility of stocks is also affected when important announcements by regulatory authorities are made or when there an outcome of a lawsuit is declared. That is why I always ask you to keep an eye out for these incidences if you want to narrow down on which stocks you should invest and which you shouldn't.

Implied volatility charts can be accessed on several options trading platforms, and this somehow lessens your work. If you do not know what implied volatility is, well it is just a projection of volatility, but the graph is plotted with respect to the current time. But for this discussion, you can consider the two entities, that is, volatility and implied volatility, the same. But if we are to speak theoretically, then there are some minor differences between these two terms. These differences will be relevant to you only when you move on to a much-advanced stage and not before.

Now, if you are wondering what things you should check on an implied volatility chart, then allow me to explain to you. One of the good bets is to check when there has been a dip to historic lows. If you notice that there has been a dip that is comparable to one of the historic lows, then you should take note of this. There will be a bounce at this point because the traders will definitely pick on it. When the volume has reached this level, you can efficiently implement the straddle strategy.

As you might know, resistant and support techniques are two of the most important techniques to use in the case of a price chart, and they are equally important in this case too. But yes, price patterns and indicators are not required because that will be nothing but overkill.

In order to implement this strategy, you don't have to worry about anything because it is quite simple. Figure out the money call and the money put, and you have to buy closest to it. All you have to do after this is wait and watch to see what moves the market has in either direction. Now, if the prediction of your volatility readings turns out to be correct, then you will notice that the price of one leg goes way beyond the unprofitable leg so you will safely cover the price that was required to buy that unprofitable leg.

Strangles

I know that the name definitely sounds grisly, but the strategy is very easy and popular too. In the previous strategy, that is, the straddles, you saw how the market direction and the force with which the movement occurs can be used in trading options effectively, but here, you are going to learn something different.

The first step in the case of strangles is you have to predict which of the stocks can display an explosive move very soon or in the near future. If you see the implied volatility charts of these stocks, then you will see that they display some historic lows and thus, they might be having some special event like a merger, takeover, or something else. There is a difference between a stock that is strangle worthy and the one that is straddle worthy and it is – for the strangle worthy stocks, the volatility is much more.

Your main aim would be to look out for those stocks that might show a certain movement in a direction rather explosively. If you compare the success rates of a strangle and a straddle, then I would say that the strangle definitely has a lower rate of success, but since the amount is more than average, so it will compensate for you in that respect. Moreover, you require a far lesser amount to enter a strangle than you need with a straddle. This is mainly because, in the case of strangles, you are basically trading with out-of-the-money options.

Iron Condor

There are two categories for this particular strategy – short and long. But it is not so simple like that. There are some complicated things which I am going to explain to you here. If you are able to apply the iron condor strategy successfully, then you are working two separate strategies for strangle in two different positions, that is – long and short. Thus, as you can understand, the implementation of the strategy is done through several puts and calls. You will have to either sell or buy calls or puts, and all of them should have the same date of expiration and must be out-of-the-money. The order should be from lowest to highest. So, you will be doing something like this – sell a put, purchase a put, sell a call, purchase a call.

Investors who predict that the market is going to stay neutral in the upcoming days are the ones who implement this strategy. The net credit received is the maximum profit potential in the case of an iron condor. The put spread and the call spread in the case of an iron condor should have the same width. An example should make it clearer. If there is a 10 points gap between the strike prices of the call options, then there should be an equal 10 points gap between the strike prices of the put options as well. But you should also note that the gap between the put and the calls is not of any significance here. You do not have to worry about bearish or bullish bias while using the iron condor strategy.

Now, let us move on to the discussion as to how an iron condor can help you make money and how it can make you lose money as well. The hope of every investor when they have an iron condor is that the trading range of the underlying securities should remain relatively narrow for the entire duration of the trade. So, when the expiration date approaches, all the options should remain out-of-the-money, and only then they will expire without any worth, and this will give you profit because you get to keep all the money you collected. The commissions will have to be subtracted from this. Yes, it is true that you will not get the ideal situation at all times but it is also true that it will happen from time to time and you simply have to utilize that situation to its full capacity.

You should keep in mind that sometimes the last few nickels have to be sacrificed so that you can take home the major potential profit without losing the money that you have already made. You also have to keep in mind that options are for short-term trading, and there is an expiration date before which you have to close your position. Once you do that, you will be eliminating any scope of unlimited losses and also lock in a substantial amount of profit. That is why one of the most essential skills that every trader needs to possess is that of managing risk, and I am going to explain this topic further in Chapter 10. You will need those risk management tips when you are using the iron condor strategy.

The prices of the securities are very volatile since the market will not be accommodating in the same manner at all times. And if that happens, then you will be witnessing a price change in the underlying assets of your options. If you consider your position, then a price change might not be good for you. So, how much can your losses amount to? Let us assume that you are selling spreads of ten-points. Now, if both the calls and puts become in-the-money by a huge movement in stocks before the expiration date, then the maximum amount has been achieved by the spread, and it is equivalent to a hundred times the difference between strike prices.

Depending on the underlying assets of your options, there are a few circumstances that you should know about, and these are as follows –

- The loss potential can be reduced, but with that, the profit potential is also reduced (you have to choose options that are further out-of-the-money)

- In order to increase the profit potential, the probability of occurrence of profit is reduced (you have to choose options that are less out-of-the-money)

- You will have to perform a bit of trial and error in order to find options that are completely in your comfort zone. That I why, I always advise beginners to stick with sectors or indices that you are completely aware of and have an in-depth understanding about.

Naked Calls

In this type of options strategy, you (as an investor) do not own any underlying security, but you are selling the call options in the open market. There are some other terms that are used to refer to this strategy, and they are short call or uncovered call.

With this strategy, you get the chance to make some profits, but you do not own the underlying security. The main motive for selling an uncovered call option is the premium that you receive. It is definitely a very risky strategy to use since the profit potential is very limited, and on the other side, the loss potential or the downside is unlimited.

The maximum profit that you can make in this type of strategy is the premium. You receive this premium upfront, and it gets credited to your account. So, do you know what your goal is? Your goal, as the seller, would be to make the option expire without any worth. The maximum loss, in this case, has no limits at all because if you think theoretically, then the underlying security's price can rise as high as it wants. But if we were to think practically, then chances are that the options will be bought back by the seller and that too before the underlying security's price goes way above the strike price and this will depend on two things which are – the stop-loss settings and the risk tolerance of the investor.

The breakeven point for the seller in the case of the naked calls is calculated by adding the strike price, and the premium received. If the implied volatility shows a rise, then it is not good for the seller as the tendency of the options to be in-the-money rises, and so they have a higher tendency to be exercised now. Since the goal of the option seller is to allow the naked calls to expire while they are out-of-the-money, the strategy will be impacted by the factor of time decay. You also need to remember that the risk potential for this strategy is unlimited and so the margin requirements are also very high.

Exit Strategies

Before you start trading, one of the most important things to figure out is your exit strategy so that you do not have to bear any huge losses. Until and unless you have figure out your exit strategy, you should not jump into a trade just like that. Before the expiration date approaches, you can choose to close or exit your trade any time you want, but the time at which you exit plays a pivoting role in the trade. The exit point is basically the point that separates a successful trade from an unsuccessful one.

Closing Out

One of the exit strategies is to close out on the option. This can be done in two ways, which I am going to explain to you here. One of the ways in which you can do it is by selling the option that you bought, and the other way is to purchase the option that you sold. In short, you simply have to reverse your position. You will make a profit when the premium goes up after you have purchased the option. On the contrary, you need to take measures to diminish your losses and sell the option if the premium has decreased.

You will never be under the obligation of purchasing the underlying security of an option as a seller because you always have the scope of closing out your position before the option is exercised.

But here too, the timing will play a big role. That is why you can never lose track of your investments. You should always be monitoring them closely so that you know when the time to sell has arrived. You will also know whether you have to take measures to cut your losses or whether you have to collect your profits. Your options will become more and more volatile as the expiration date approaches, and that is also when you need to keep an eye on them even more closely.

Rolling Out

You can also choose to roll out your options if you don't want to close out. This means that you have to open a new position after you have closed out your previous position. But this new position should be the same as the position you closed. The only difference should be the expiration date or the strike or both.

Exercising the Options

You can opt to exercise the options if you are the options holder, and then you will have to purchase the underlying security of that option. But this will work out in your favor only when the options are in-the-money because if the case is either of the other two scenarios, then it will not work out in your favor. If you are the seller, then you cannot control the exercising of that option by the buyer.

These were the possible exit strategies that you can choose, and once you have figured out which one to choose, you need to monitor the trades and then stick to the plan. It is very easy for you to get caught up in the moment or get distracted in options trading because of its fast-paced nature. So, you should not let your emotions get the better of you. If you follow your plan with due diligence, you will surely witness the profits growing over a period of time.

But another thing that you should be aware of despite all these strategies is over-trading. There will be times when you are not trading, and you will feel as if you are missing out on all the profits that you could have collected during that time. But you have to remind yourself that something that is happening in the market is not always worth chasing and so it is completely okay to take a break and moreover, it is necessary especially if you have had successive wins or losses. Both can make you feel overwhelmed and cloud your mind preventing you from making the right decisions.

Everything that has been mentioned in this chapter should be enough to help you take your first step in the world of options trading. You will learn more and more with time and experience. Also, stop comparing yourself with seasoned traders because they are where they are today because they have spent years in this field and not one or two months.

Chapter 8
AN EXAMPLE OF HOW OPTIONS TRADING WORKS

Now that you have learned all the basics and some strategies, let me give you a few examples to revise all that you have learned. The two examples that I have given here should further clarify any doubts that you might have regarding the call and put options.

But first, to make it simpler, here are some things that we are assuming –

- Stock price during writing an option - $100

- Expiration date – Within 1 month of buying the option

- Premium - $5

Case – 1

In this case, the current stock price is $110, and the strike price is $120.

Type of Option	Moneyness	Owner	Result
Call	Out-of-the-money	Buyer	If the buyer decides to purchase the stock from the seller, the amount that the buyer has to pay is $125 ($5 + $120)
			The buyer is most likely to not exercise this option at all because they are better off purchasing the stock directly.
Call	Out-of-the-	Seller	The seller is going to

	money		make a profit since the buyer is not exercising the option, and the total profit is limited to the premium paid.
Put	In-the-money	Buyer	The stock can be sold by the options buyer at $120, which will earn them profits amounting to $115 ($120 - $5), and this is greater than the stock price, that is, $110. Thus, the put option will be exercised by the buyer.

| Put | In-the-money | Seller | Now, if the put option is carried out, there will be a loss for the seller amounting to $5 ($120 - $110 - $5) |

Case – 2

In this case, let us consider that the stock price is $120, and the strike price of that stock is $110.

Type of Option	Moneyness	Owner	Result
Call	In-the-money	Buyer	If the buyer decides to purchase the stock from the seller, the amount that the buyer has to pay is $115 ($5 + $110)
			The buyer is going to exercise the option because they are going to make a profit of $5 when they sell that stock after buying it at $120, which

			is the current price.
Call	In-the-money	Seller	When the buyer exercises the option, the seller will incur a loss amounting to $5 ($120 - $110 - $5)
Put	Out-of-the-money	Buyer	The stock could be sold in the market at a price of $120 by the option buyer instead of selling to the seller at $110 which was the strike price agreed upon
			In simpler terms, the option

			expires, and the buyer incurs a loss of $5, that is, the same amount as the premium paid.
Put	Out-of-the-money	Seller	Since the put option was not carried out, the seller incurs a profit of $5, that is, the same amount as the premium paid.

CHAPTER 9
TIPS TO KEEP IN MIND IF YOU WANT TO BECOME A TOP TRADER

If you want to become successful as a top trader in options trading, I am going to give you some tips on how you can do that. Mistakes are common with people, but with some prior knowledge, you can easily avoid them.

Know When to Improvise Your Plan

While having a plan in options trading is of utmost importance, another thing that is very much important is to know when your plan needs some improvisation. There will be times when you have to move away from your plan, even when your emotions are telling you to stick to it. A successful trader knows when their plan is no longer valid for the current situation. Having a plan sets your path, but this does not mean that you will follow it blindly to the end of the world. Every trader comes to a point where something totally out of their control happens, and this renders their plan useless for that situation.

That is why, when you make a plan, know what its weak points are and when it can fail. The conditions in the market keep changing constantly, so what is true today might not be applicable tomorrow. So, if you are thinking of following your predetermined course of action even when the conditions of the market have taken a 360-degree turn, then you are making a big mistake. This will only lead you to your failure. Yes, it will require a lot of practice to understand when it is your emotions that are holding you back and when the situations are changing. But every small step in the right direction is progress, and this includes being aware of the disparity.

Always Have Your Exit and Entry Plan Ready Before Starting

When it comes to options trading, figuring out the right entries and exits is probably one of the things that you should learn well. No matter how good your adjustment techniques are, nothing can correct a bad entry, and you might end up incurring huge losses because of that.

But there is something else that is even more important that learning to set the right entry and exit points. Can you guess what it is? Well, it is about understanding the fact that you have to exercise your entry and exit points before the money is off the table. New options traders have this idea that every trade has to fetch your huge profits and you need every last cent out of it. But you have to break free from this mentality. This can pose a big hurdle for every new trader. As long as you have a trading plan that is solid and profitable, there will be several trades in the future that can fetch you profits. So, sticking to only one of them as if it is the last trade you are going to perform is wrong, and it will only end up in giving you a loss.

So, stop worrying about those small extra profits because you have already made a certain amount of profit from a trade and now you have to protect that. Yes, there is a chance that if you ignore this advice and continue with your trading mentality, you might make a few extra bucks here and there, but the odds are that the loss will be more than the gain. You will end up losing the profit you made without even getting the chance to pull the trigger.

Avoid Out-of-the-Money Trades

There are a few strategies that can help you make a profit even by buying out-of-the-money call options, but they are certainly the exception. You, as a new investor in options trading, might feel attracted to the out-of-the-money call options because they are affordable and cheap, but you need to remind yourself that the stock market and the options market are two different scenarios. Even if you look at the underlying stocks to buy the options, it is not a viable strategy to simply buy low and then sell high. In case a call has become out-of-the-money, then there is very little chance for it to again rise up to the required levels before it approaches its expiration date. So, if you still buy these options, then you are just a step away from gambling with your money.

Don't Shrink Your Homework

There are so many instances where options traders lose sides just because they did not perform their homework. If you ask the new traders, you will often find that they are guilty of not performing extensive and adequate research of the market. They even fail to possess due diligence before making a trade. Do you know why I am stressing so much about performing your homework properly? Well, if you don't, then you will never be aware of the timing of the data releases, the seasonal trends, or trading patterns, all of which are something that experienced traders are aware of. New traders are so overwhelmed with the idea of making a trade as soon as possible that they do not think it is ideal to do some research, and then this turns out to be quite an expensive lesson for them.

Even if you are not interested in an investment, you should still take some time out to research it. When you perform thorough research, you will get to know everything about a particular financial statement, and you will also be fully aware of the path you are treading on. For example, if you decide to invest in options, then you need to do research on the various strategies that you can apply. Remember that every other trader has access to the same information as you, so if you give the effort, then even you can identify the investments that will give good results.

You should also make a promise to yourself t that you are going to read at least one new book on options trading every week. When you read books, you learn a lot of secrets, and you also learn a lot of new things. You will also acquire a deeper knowledge of the rewards and risks involved in options trading.

Don't Trade for Wealth But for Income

If you think that options trading is going to give you returns like 150%, then you need to take a step back and reconsider. Yes, it is true that there might be certain investments once in a while that will give you such figures, but not every trade is like that. Most new traders think that options trading is going to make them rich overnight but there is no such thing as that.

If you believe that you are doing options trading for wealth generation, then you have got it all wrong. It is more like devising the right strategy to get a regular income. If you become hungry for more profits, then it is more likely for you to overlook the risky endeavors and invest your money anyway. Never forget that options trading can be full of risks, so you have to take your steps carefully.

Never Believe in Unfounded Tips

Another very common mistake that new traders make is that they start believing in random tips. This mistake is made by almost every trader at some point or the other in their life. It might be that one of your friends or relatives has been going on discussing a certain company whose stocks are performing well, and maybe they are going to make a groundbreaking profit by investing in that stock. What you should do is do your own research before believing anything. I am not saying whatever they are saying is false. It can be true, but that does not mean you have to pounce on it right away as if it is the next big thing and you are going to lose it if you do not go for it now. Take a step back before rushing to your online brokerage right now and do your research.

The above-mentioned example is of only one source of unfounded tips. Another one comes from social media and television. You will often find investment professionals on both these media who can't stop talking about a particular stock as it is a must investment, but if you probe into the matter deeply, you will find that it has nothing extraordinary about it. You have to remind yourself that if you keep following media tips, it is nothing more than a speculative gamble in the world of trading.

But all this talk about unfounded tips does not mean you should turn a blind eye to every tip that you receive. If there is something that has really caught your attention and you can't let go of it, then your first task would be to think whether the source is reliable or not. The next step is definitely performing your own homework, and this will give you the information you need. So, don't rely on anyone telling you what to do. You need to figure out whether or not that will be the right type of investment for you. You can also look for a second opinion from someone who is reliable and unbiased.

Start With Enough Capital

Although it is true that you do not really need much capital to start, it is also true that you should have enough capital to get you set up. In simpler terms, capital is the amount of money that you should keep in your trading account so that you can clear any money required for the transactions, and this same capital will help you if you incur a loss during trading.

Your trading account should always have some amount of money in it. This is because when you are making trades, you should not worry yourself with things like funds transfer, and the money already being present in your account means things are going to work out smoothly. Your broker can also help you out without any delay from fund transfer. If you ask the successful traders in the market, all of them will say the same thing. They always keep some money in their account and keep checking their balance from time to time so that even if they have a few bad trades in the future, the money in the account will act as a cushion for them.

Don't Purchase Too Much With Margin

The meaning of 'margin' was explained at the beginning of this book. It is when you purchase options by borrowing some money from your broker. It is true that in some cases, you can make more money with the help of margins, but on the contrary, if you face losses, they will become even more exaggerated because of the margins. So, you need to have a proper understanding of how margin works. You also need to understand that using margins also means your broker can ask you any time to sell your options.

New traders often get carried away because they think margins mean free money so they keep using it until the nightmare comes. For example, suppose you have used margin, but then the investment went south. This would mean that you are left with a huge debt obligation to the broker and that too, for nothing because you did not get any profits at all. It is somewhat similar to buying options with your credit card. Would you do that? No, right? It is the same thing when you use margins excessively.

You also need to keep a close eye on your positions if you are using margins. When you have exaggerated losses or gains along with price movements that are really small, you are stepping into a disaster. In case you do not have the required knowledge or time to monitor your positions or make decisions about them, then you are at risk because in case the values drop, your assets will be sold by the firm so that they can accrue the losses they have incurred.

So, as a new trader, I would advise you to stay away from margins. If you are using them at all, then make sure you know what you are doing.

Don't Keep All Your Eggs in One Basket

You should never overexpose yourself to any single form of investment, and this brings me to our next point – diversification is the key to success. It will be a rookie mistake if you have not diversified your portfolio. When your portfolio is diversified, you won't be losing a lot of money even if one of the investments brings you losses. Diversification also protects you from extreme movements in the price and volatility of any particular investment option. Moreover, there will times when one of the asset classes in underperforming but when your portfolio is diversified, there will always be another asset class that is performing well.

Always Be Positive and Focused

Panic is something that is faced by new traders a lot, and if you notice that you are about to panic, you need to calm yourself down. If you want to make good trades, then you have to keep panic out of the way. You also need to understand where your exit doors are. Not understanding this is also one of the reasons why people start panicking in the first place. Now that you have learned about most of the tips that can bring you profits, it is also important to understand that you need to stay focused. If you cannot avoid panic and stay focused, you will be missing out on the right time to trade.

There are so many people who think that options trading is one of the easiest things to do, and everyone can do it. They literally jump in and depend on luck for profits. But that is not the right way to do it. If you practice this method, you are bound to become overwhelmed by the process, and chances are that you are now aware of what you are dealing with. I know that if you are not used to options trading, it will seem a bit confusing and difficult at first but you can always learn it and be an expert.

If you already have problems focusing, then try things like meditation to enhance your power of focusing. If you cannot focus, then options trading is not going to be the right form of investment for you because you will miss out on important things. If you are able to keep your focus on this trading style, you are surely going to make profits from it. Trust yourself and restrain from following the crowd. There may be times when people around you are making profits and you are not and you will be thinking that maybe following them is what is going to bring you profits. But that is just a misconception. You need to learn to trust your own judgment. It is only you who knows goals, aspirations, and risk appetite and it might not match with someone else. So, you need to follow the plan that suits you.

Chapter 10
HOW TO MINIMIZE YOUR RISKS?

There will always be risks, and you simply have to learn to manage them and minimize them as much as possible. Your aim should definitely be how you can make huge profits on the trades. There is some risk associated with every investment you make and options are no different. The risk tolerance threshold of every person is different and there is nothing wrong with that. You should not force yourself and stretch too thin otherwise; you will be the one left with nothing. Trading should always be done with that money which you can afford to lose. Although options trading has a lot of benefits, they also have great risks and in this chapter, you will learn how you can reduce those risks.

Diversify Your Portfolio

Arranging your portfolio should be done with care because it can really help you in minimizing your risks to a great extent. In order to protect your portfolio, you need to diversify your investments. The idea is very simple. When there are multiple investments in a portfolio, it has lower risk since it poses higher returns, especially when compared to a portfolio containing individual investments only. One way of doing it is to choose the investments that differ in their rate of returns. You can also choose to invest in different sectors and not put all your investments in a single sector.

Always Have a Plan

If you want to take options trading seriously, then it is extremely necessary to have a plan. This plan should have all the steps that you want to take and everything that you want to do. It would be even better if you write it all down. There are some beginners who go all in and they literally jump into the trade without knowing much about it. They have this attitude where they want to make as much money as they can but let me tell you something – this is an absolutely horrible strategy to follow. This is because the plan does not involve any strategy at all and you do not have any enter or exit plan in the trade. Basically, nothing is in place. If you are of the idea that you are going to wing it with options trading then trust me, you better give up now; otherwise, you are going to face huge losses.

So, when you make the plan, make sure that you have

made it as detailed as possible. The first thing that you have to figure out is your expectation regarding how much profit you want to make through options trading. But this does not mean jotting down whatever figure comes to your mind. You have to be realistic about your expectations. In the first year of options trading, you are not going to make millions so quit having such high expectations. Another thing that you can do is make a note of all the things that are required when you decide to buy an option, and you should also note down what you want to see in each of those options.

Next, you can make a list of the strategies you want to implement. By now, you must have realized that there are tons of strategies that can be used, but what you will be using will depend on the type of situation you are in. The strategy also depends on the option you have chosen. Remember that it is not necessary for you to keep working with one single option throughout and if you change them in the right situation, then you can even have the chance of making more money, especially if you consider the long term. But do you know why I am asking you to write down the strategies? It is because of a very simple reason and that is – when you write down the strategies, they automatically become simpler and you can keep track of them in the same place. It will also help you make more money by choosing the right options.

Another thing to keep in mind is that you always need to have an exit strategy. And you need to figure it out before you even step into a trade. For starters, you need to think as to how much money you are actually willing to lose, or rather you can afford to lose. You also need to make a note of the conditions during which you will step out of the trade at all costs. Do you know what happens to those who do not have this information in place? They lose a lot of money simply because they do not know when to exit from a trade and they keep going even when it costs them everything. This happens mostly when someone is doing well and so giving up or leaving at the right time becomes quite difficult for them. This also happens when people stay in the trade because they are trying hard to gain back all the money that they have lost but this only makes them lose more money. So, when you have that exit strategy in place, you know what you have to do when things go south. So, having an exit strategy is truly one of the most important things in risk management.

So, now you might be feeling a bit overwhelmed because you think you have to figure out so many things before you can even start to trade. But what you need to understand is that you can take all the time you need, but you have to make sure that all this information is in place if you want to make profits from the trade. Making the right decisions will no longer seem that much tough and you will always have the path ready because you have planned it all before. You also know what your goals are so that you are not winging it. You are actually putting effort into the trade.

In case you feel confused with the process, and you are not sure whether your plan is good or not, you can consider talking with your broker. Since brokers talk with lots of people and they handle different kinds of traders, they can even help you out in framing the plan based on your requirements and expectations.

Never Skip on Research

Doing sufficient research before jumping into the world of options trading is very important. I have come across so many people in my who came into options trading just because they heard it from someone who made a big fortune, or they think that it is a very easy way of making money. There are so many people who think that they are going to get a big break overnight and they think that options trading is the best way to do so. It is true that with options trading, you can make some handsome amount of money but it is also true that you need to devote your time and effort and wait patiently before you get handsome results.

Doing your research thoroughly is very important, and you can call it a prerequisite of making a profit in the world of options trading. And if you are a beginner, it means that you have to do a lot of research because you start with nothing. But don't worry, once you start the research, everything will start falling into place. You need to learn different ways of studying the market and you also need to understand how to figure out the best time to invest in the market. Then, you also have to learn different strategies and know when to use what. But yes, in the beginning, you have to start by learning what options are and what is the difference between options and other forms of investments in the stock market. If you have read the previous chapters, then you have already covered these things.

There is basically no end to the amount of research you can do. So, take your time and learn it step by step. Don't rush into it and understand everything that you learn. Only then can you stay in the world of options trading in the long-term.

Learn to Manage Your Emotions

I have already devoted an entire chapter explaining how important it is to learn to manage your emotions, and I have repeated it many times throughout this book. Whenever you let your emotions interfere with your trading strategies, you are bound to make mistakes, and things will go south. You might even end up losing all your money. Would you like that? No, right? Then, it is high time that you learn to manage your emotions effectively. Emotions have to be managed regardless of what plan you are following or what strategies you have in place. Even if you are doing well now does not mean that you will not become emotional tomorrow. So, learning to manage emotions is a basic lesson for options trading.

Emotions have the tendency to force people into making decisions that will work against them and make them lose money. It can be in any form. Sometimes people stay in the market more than it is necessary and sometimes, people leave too early and both these situations can make you lose money. Also, every successful trader has gone through a phase where they became emotional, but in the end, they learned to control themselves. So, even if you became emotional this one time, there is no need to beat yourself up for it. Learn from your mistakes and then grow from there. You cannot let your emotions control your decisions; otherwise making profits will become impossible.

If you have this basic nature of being too stubborn or emotional, then options trading is something that you should not consider right now. In this form of trading, you have to stick to the plan if you want things to work out in your favor. So, if you think you cannot do that and you might become impulsive then work on dealing with that first before you enter options trading. At times, options trading can get really emotional causing you to become overwhelmed, panicked, or even too happy from the profits you made. There are some people who are inherently good at managing their emotions and it comes naturally to them, but not everyone is like that. So, before you go in and risk all your savings, it is time to ask yourself what kind of person you really are and are you suitable to dive into options trading right now?

Always Keep an Eye on the Features Offered By Your Broker

Some people think that the broker is only the person who will perform some trades and help you with things you cannot understand, but there is a lot more to it than this. There will be times when you did not make the right call, but your broker might be able to help you out of the situation in some ways.

One of the ways in which brokers can help you is by providing an out-of-the-money rate. Options trading has a major drawback, that is, at times, people have the possibility of losing their entire money, but when your broker offers you out-of-the-money rates, then you will not go entirely broke and manage to get some of the money back. This is basically an agreement that the investor will make with the broker where the broker agrees to pay a certain amount of money invested back to the investor. It is true that you will still lose some money, but at least you will not lose it all.

But you also have to keep in mind that this feature is not provided by every broker in the market, so you have to keep an eye out on who is providing what. Don't settle for the first option you come across. There is another way in which brokers can help you and that is by giving the sell back feature. This is a feature that you can avail when you are about to incur a loss because you made a bad call. With the help of this feature, you will be able to exit before the options approach their expiration date. Of course, if you leave the trade early, up to 60% of your initial investment is lost, but it also means that you will not lose everything.

Manage Your Money Efficiently

I know you must be thinking that managing money is something everyone should do whether they are doing options trading or not, and I totally agree with you, but this is also something most people tend to overlook. So, I couldn't help but mention this in this chapter of risk management. There are some people who simply cannot figure it out as to how they are going to manage their money. Well, for starters, you have to figure out a way in which you make the least amount of losses. In case you are a person who doesn't have good money management skills in day-to-day life, then I am sorry to say that options trading is not for you.

There will be both good and bad times in trade, and you will have to know how you can manage your money in both these situations. The first thing that you have to learn is to come up with a full-proof plan for managing the money. You also need to understand that losing is something that can happen to anyone, be it a beginner or an expert. It can be a series of losses or it can also be just one loss. This is mostly because the market is never stagnant and it keeps changing from time to time and this is something that no human being can control. But do you know why I am asking you to realize the fact that losses are totally normal? This is because when you do that, you will be building the right mindset for the trade.

Once you understand the fact that losing money is totally normal and can happen to anyone, you will be able to walk on the path of controlling the amount of money that you can possibly lose. This is also where the importance of exit strategy comes in, as explained in the previous sections of this chapter. When you have these plans figured out right from the beginning, you will see for yourself what a big difference it can make to your trading experience. And of course, having planned it all is definitely one of the greatest determinants of success in options trading.

Always Monitor Your Trades

What I mean by this is that once you have placed your trade, you need to monitor it too. Placing orders does not end your job. Never ignore things once you have invested your money in the options. You cannot simply hope that one fine day you will wake up and find that you are a millionaire. No, it does not happen like that. You always need to keep track of how your trades are performing.

Monitor your chosen option and see how it is performing. This will also ensure that you are able to make smart decisions. You will know when you need to hold on to it or when you need to sell it so that you can minimize your losses or maximize your profit. All of these things are so important, and the choices you make will directly influence your profit potential. And if you do not keep track of your trades and monitor them, how are you going to know whether they are performing well or not?

CONCLUSION

Thank you for making it through to the end of Options Trading for Beginners: The Step-By-Step Crash Course To Make Money and Create a Passive Income by Options Trading Just a Few Minutes a Day, let's hope it was informative and able to provide you with all of the tools you need to achieve your goals whatever they may be.

I have said it multiple times since the beginning of this book that trading does not necessarily have to be a complicated subject. It is as easy or as difficult as you see it. It is just like any other form of investment. It has its own tools and strategies that you have to learn in order to master the art. So, whether you are a seasoned professional or completely new to the world of options trading, it does not matter. The only thing that you have to remember is that you need to keep learning no matter what. If you want to guarantee your financial stability in the future, options trading can serve as an effective tool for that.

I have made this book, especially for beginners, so that they can know about everything starting from the most basic terminology to some basic strategies to get you started. If you follow everything with due diligence, there is so much potential for you to grow in options and expand your horizons. But remember that you should not overcomplicate things because the more confused you become, the more your chances are of losing money.

Finally, if you found this book useful in any way, a review on Amazon is always appreciated!

www.ingramcontent.com/pod-product-compliance
Lightning Source LLC
Chambersburg PA
CBHW071413210526
45465CB00001B/359